The Changing Me

David Edens

Illustrated by Bill McPheeters

BROADMAN PRESS
Nashville, Tennessee

C. L. HARDY LIBRARY
ATLANTIC CHRISTIAN COLLEGE
WILSON, N. C. 27893

© Copyright 1973 • Broadman Press
All rights reserved
4244-11
ISBN: 0-8054-4411-4
Dewey Decimal Classification: J612.6
Printed in the United States of America

How are bananas grown?
How do rockets work?
What makes it rain?
How do human bodies work?
How does life start?
Where were you before your life started?

How many of these questions could you answer? All of them? Some of them? How would you find answers to the ones you don't know?

If you want to know how bananas grow, how a rocket works, or what makes it rain, you may ask someone who grows bananas, an astronaut or space engineer, or a weatherman who predicts rain. You may go to the library and find books that will help you discover answers.

But how do you find out how your body works and how life starts? Your parents can help you know the answers, though sometimes it's hard for parents to talk about bodies and sex and reproduction. But all of these are a part of where you were before your life started.

Not only can parents help you find the answers you need, but other adults can help you. Some of these people might be a doctor, a teacher who is a good friend, or a neighbor who is a friend.

Just as you can read books to learn about bananas, rockets, and rain, you can also read books to help you know about sex. This book is written to help you know what's happening to you as you grow and change.

Sex is important in your life from the time you are born. Sex is what makes you a boy or a girl. It describes you as a boy or a girl. Sex, or sexuality, is a part of how you feel about yourself and about others.

You have heard the word "sex" used in different ways. Sometimes it is used to talk about a person's body. Sometimes sex means what a person does with his body. Sex has more than one meaning. As boys grow older and begin to like to be with girls, and girls with boys, this interest is a part of the meaning of sex.

Boys and girls want to know about growing up. They want to think about the future. Like other boys and girls, you want to know about growing up. You probably have questions that are important to you. You may have

wondered about many ideas. But you may not know exactly how to ask your questions or how to talk about your ideas. It is important for you to ask the questions you have, especially questions about sex. It's important for you to understand and know what is true. It *is* all right to talk about sex.

The way you feel about things and about people is part of how you are growing and changing sexually. You love your parents, but sometimes you think they are unfair. You know how grown-up you are beginning to be, but parents seem to forget that you are growing. As you grow and as your body changes on its way to becoming an adult, emotions have a big job to do.

Emotions is another word for feelings. Being angry, or happy, or sad, or jealous, or afraid, or lonely are emotions. A very important feeling or emotion, is love. Everybody has feelings, or emotions. Emotions can be helpful, but sometimes they are not. Having feelings is part of being a person.

Created Male and Female

Did you ever wonder where you were before your life started? Before people existed, God planned how he would give them life. When God created people, he created man and woman, male and female, to have children. When God created men and women, he made sex a very important part of their lives.

Everyone knows that God made men and women different from one another. He did not make one better than the other. Both men and women are necessary for God's plan for people.

You are either a boy or a girl, male or female. Do you like who you are? Boys and girls are different. They are different physically. Boys are usually thought of as having strong muscles. But boys are also tender and gentle and loving, just as are girls.

Can you remember the Bible story about creation? When God created Adam, he knew that Adam needed someone to be a companion, a helper, someone to help make a family. And so God created Eve to be Adam's wife.

The Bible tells us more about God's plan for men and women in Genesis 2:24: "Therefore shall a man leave his father and his mother, and shall cleave unto his wife: and they shall be one flesh."

Right now you are not interested in marriage. If you are a boy, you probably aren't interested in girls. And if you are a girl, you probably aren't interested in boys. You are more interested in friends of your own sex. You may have a best friend, or two best friends. If you're a girl, these best friends are probably girls, and if you're a boy, your best friends are

boys. These friends are more important to you than anyone besides your family.

Having best friends like these are part of the way you are growing and changing, getting ready someday to have best friends of the opposite sex, and one day to find the person you will marry.

Some of the things you do as you grow up will help you know how to act as a man or as a woman. Sometimes men and women are expected to act differently. A married man is expected to provide by his work the food, shelter, and clothing for his wife. He also acts as protector of his home. Usually, the wife is expected to be the homemaker, adding taste to the food and beauty to the house. This is what we call having different *roles.* But the husband can also be a homemaker, and the wife may be a provider.

Whatever a person's role is, one important job is to work with a husband or wife to make a home in which children can be born and grow to be the best persons they can be.

Not all parents are alike. Not all families are alike. You may know families where there is a father and a mother and children. Or you may know families where there is a father and a mother but no children. Or, you may know families where there is a father and children but no mother. Or maybe there is a family with a mother and children but no father. Maybe you know families that have a grandmother or a grandfather or both in the family. All families are not alike.

All children are not alike. But all children are alike in one way. They grow and change. Some grow faster than others. Some grow slower than others. Some change quickly. Some change more slowly. But all are growing and changing some.

Family members need each other. Fathers need mothers and mothers need fathers. Chil-

dren need mothers and fathers, and mothers and fathers need children.

They need one another when they watch the changing colors of a sunset, laugh together about a playful puppy, enjoy the adventure of reading, and work together in the yard or on a campsite. They also need one another when Mother gets sick, when Billy sprains his ankle while playing ball, and when Sue is teased at school about something that was not her fault.

The Wonder of the Body

You know how important families are. Perhaps you are still wondering how you became a part of yours. How did your life begin?

When your life started, you were smaller than the period at the end of this sentence. How much do you weigh now? Do you weigh sixty pounds? ninety pounds? or more? You've come a long way from the beginning, but you are still growing.

Your body now contains trillions of *cells*. But at one time you were only one cell. Two parts were needed to make this one cell: from your father, one part called a *sperm* and from your mother one part called an *egg*.

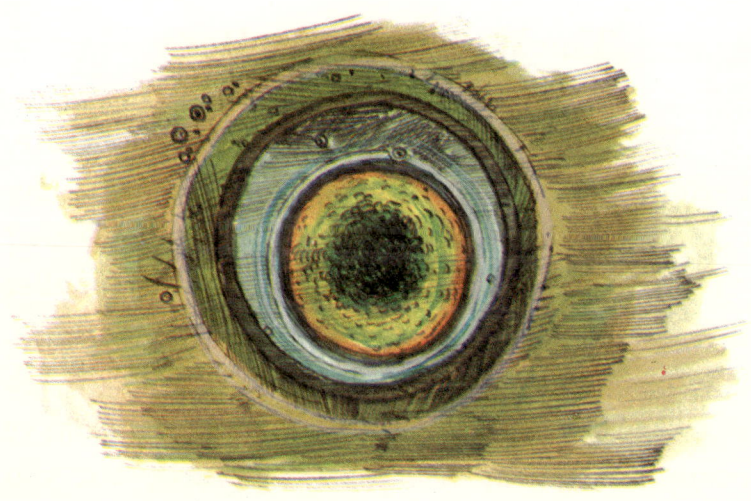

(When you see italicized words, look them up in the glossary on page 47 to be sure you understand them.)

All living things are made of cells. But the human body has about ten trillion cells. Different kinds of cells make up the skin, bones, blood, nerves, and muscles. The human body also has *reproductive* cells. These cells are different in men and in women. In men, the reproductive cells are called sperm cells. In women, they are called egg cells. A new life starts when a sperm cell from the father comes together with an egg cell from the mother.

The egg cells in a mother are all of one kind. But a father's body makes two different kinds of sperm cells. Sometimes they are called *X* cells and *Y* cells. If an *X* cell joins with an egg from the mother, a baby girl will be formed. But if a *Y* sperm cell from the father joins with an egg cell from the mother, there will be a baby boy.

Sometimes when a *fertilized* egg cell (an egg cell from the mother and a sperm cell from

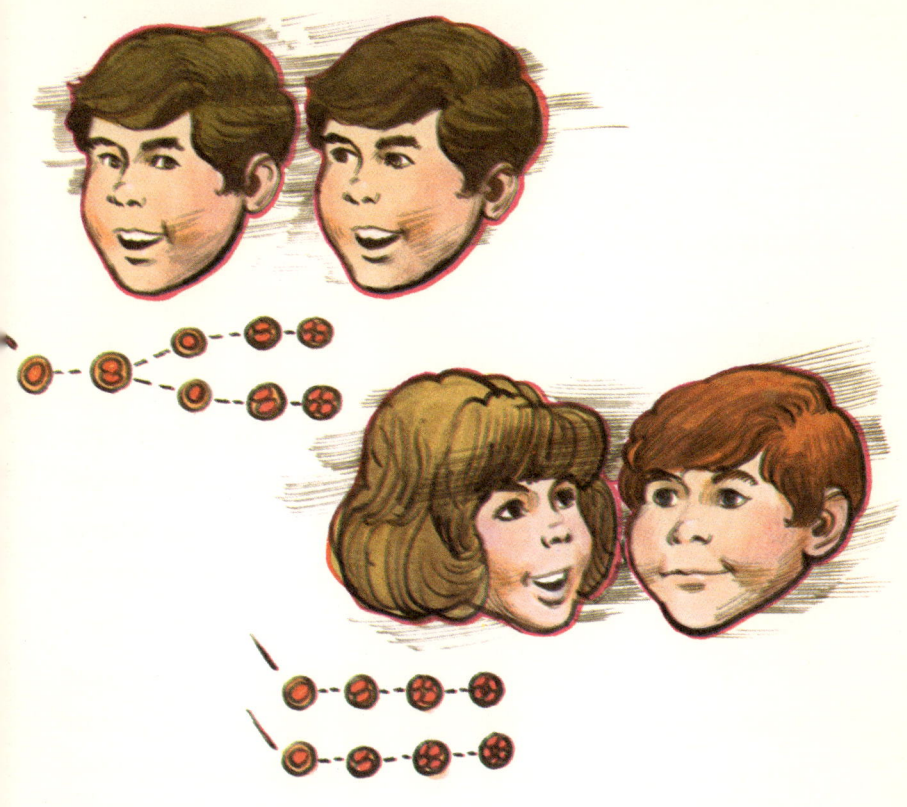

the father joined) starts to grow, it divides. Then two babies grow instead of one. These babies are called twins. You may be a twin or you may know some twins.

Twins who are born when one cell divides and two babies grow are called identical twins. They will both be boys or they will both be girls. They will look alike. But as they grow, each will grow in his own way.

Sometimes there are twins who are not identical. Then they are called fraternal twins. Fraternal twins begin to grow when two egg cells in the mother's body and two sperm cells from the father's body come together at the same time. These twins may not look alike and one may be a boy and the other a girl.

God, the Creator

Your life began one day when an egg cell and a sperm cell came together to make a fertilized egg. How does this happen?

Creating new life is God's work. But he gave men and women a share in it. It is God's plan that the husband and wife show their love to each other in a very special way. This way is called *sexual intercourse*. It is God's plan that through sexual intercourse, with a feeling of love, new life begins.

In God's plan, children are born because of love and are brought up with love from their parents. This kind of love is a very special love. It is a kind of love that will forgive a wrong-doer, the kind that is unselfish. It is a kind of love that can help children learn something of what God's love is like. Parents want children to grow up to be healthy and strong and happy. And so does God.

Men and women are created different from each other so that each one plays a different part in creating a new life. Their sex organs, the parts of their bodies that do the work of helping create new life, are different. Boys are born with sex organs that will make sperm. Girls are born with sex organs that make egg cells. At birth girls already have in their bodies partly grown egg cells.

A Mother's Sex Organs

When your mother was born, like all baby girls, she had two body parts called *ovaries* for storing egg cells. Each ovary is about the size and shape of an unshelled almond. Each ovary is small, but thousands of eggs are stored there. When a girl is around eleven to thirteen years of age, her body has changed until the egg cells begin to ripen or mature. About once a month, an egg cell leaves one or the other ovary. This is called *ovulation.*

What happens to the egg when it leaves the ovary? It leaves the ovary near a tube called the *Fallopian tube.* There is a tube for each ovary. The egg travels through the tube to the *uterus.* Most of the eggs fall apart by the time they reach the uterus. All this time, the uterus has been getting ready for the egg. The inside of the uterus has become thicker and softer because there is more blood in it.

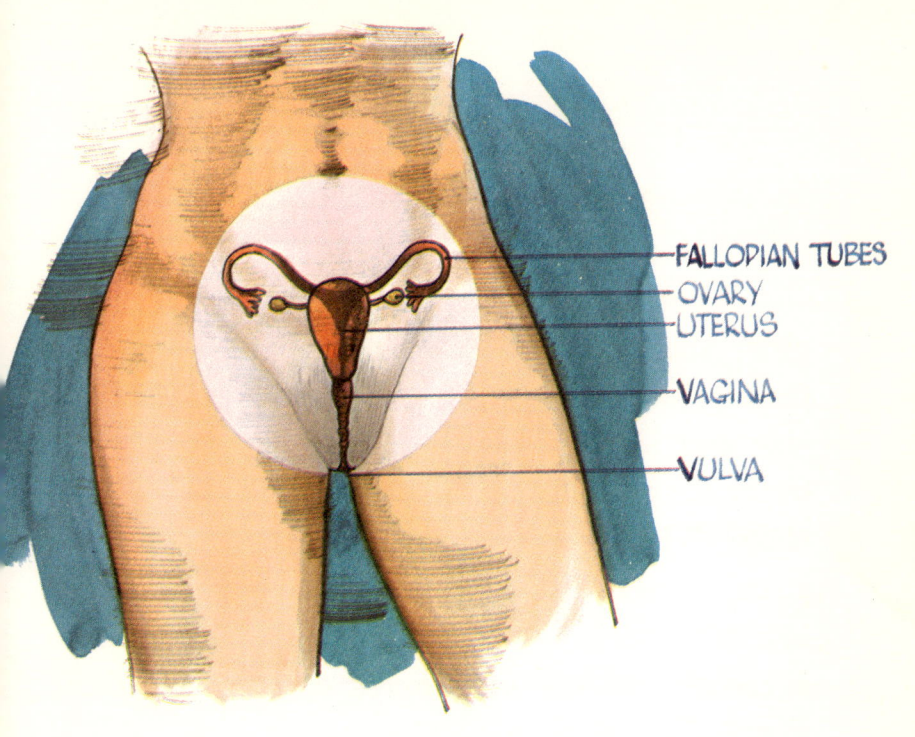

When the egg is not fertilized (does not join with a sperm cell), the lining of the uterus is not needed and it breaks apart. Then *menstruation* occurs. Menstruation is really the discharge of a small amount of blood from the uterus through the *vagina*. A woman expects menstruation to happen about once every month. When it does, she knows her body is working right.

But what happens if a sperm cell from the father joins the egg cell after it leaves the ovary? The fertilized egg goes on through the Fallopian tube until it reaches the uterus. Then it fastens itself to the wall of the uterus. A baby then begins to grow. For nine months, a baby grows inside the mother in her uterus. Here the baby has all the food and protection he needs for nine months.

The uterus is connected to the outside of the body by a narrow passageway. This passageway expands to allow the baby to be born. This passageway is called the vagina and opens between the legs.

The ovaries, the tubes, the uterus, and the vagina are the reproductive organs of the female. They are inside the body.

A Father's Sex Organs

The father's sex organs are the two *testicles* and the *penis*. The testicles produce the sperm cells and are in a sac of skin outside the body. The sac hangs between the legs and is called the *scrotum*.

Sperm are smaller than egg cells. Billions of sperm are produced each month and are

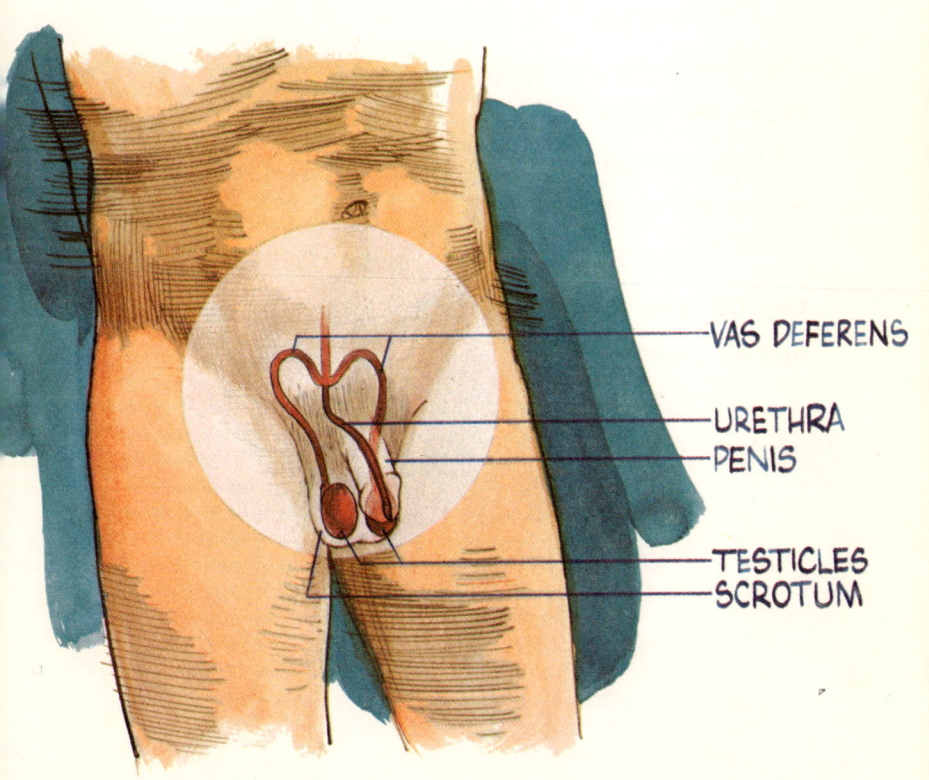

stored in a tube in the testicles. This tube leads to the outside through the penis, a finger-shaped organ which hangs in front of the testicles. It is usually soft and limp, but it can become firm and stand out from the body. This is called an *erection.*

When a boy is born, the end of his penis is partly covered by loose skin. A doctor can cut this away in a simple operation called circumcision. Circumcision will help a boy keep this part of his body clean.

When a boy is about thirteen to fifteen, his body is ready to make mature sperm cells. His body also makes a whitish fluid. The sperm and this fluid together are called *semen.* When semen is discharged in the vagina of a woman, the sperm can begin their journey to find an egg cell.

Love Brought You to Life

The act that brings a man's sperm cells and a woman's egg cells together is sexual intercourse. When a husband and a wife are alone and want to show their special love for each other, they often lie close together, embracing and kissing each other. The man's penis becomes firm and erect and can fit into the woman's vagina, which is soft and stretches easily. This allows the man to release his semen inside the woman. If there is an egg cell in the tubes when the sperm gets there, one sperm joins with the egg and *conception* happens—a baby begins to grow.

When a husband and wife show love like this, they both get much pleasure from it. This is one of God's ways of continuing his creation today. He uses the love of husband and wife to bring children into the world.

Sexual intercourse is only one part of the love between husband and wife. But intercourse is a very important part of marriage. It gives great pleasure, and the husband and wife have intercourse because they enjoy it as well as because they want to have children.

Sometimes a husband and wife are not physically able to have a baby of their own. They may then adopt a baby who was born to parents who cannot care for it.

The First Nine Months

For nine months you grew in your mother's uterus or *womb*. (Look in the glossary if you forget what the italicized words mean.) You were in a sac of liquid in the uterus where you were protected and fed. During this time your mother was *pregnant*.

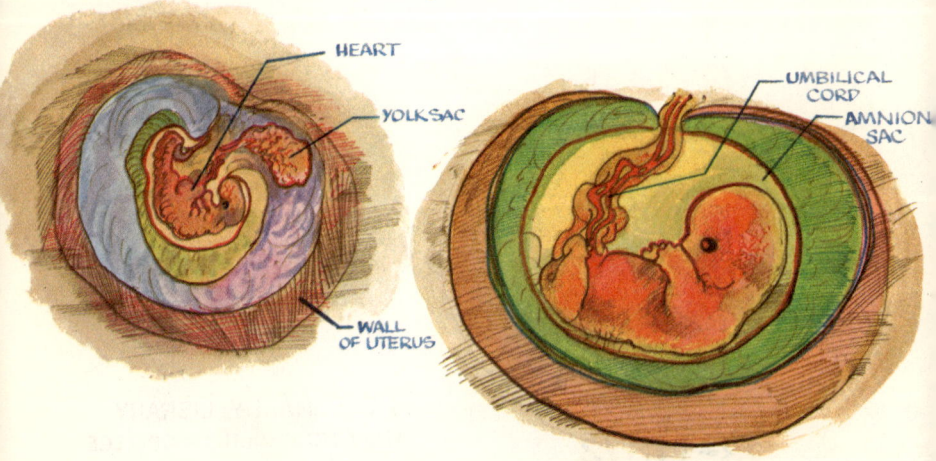

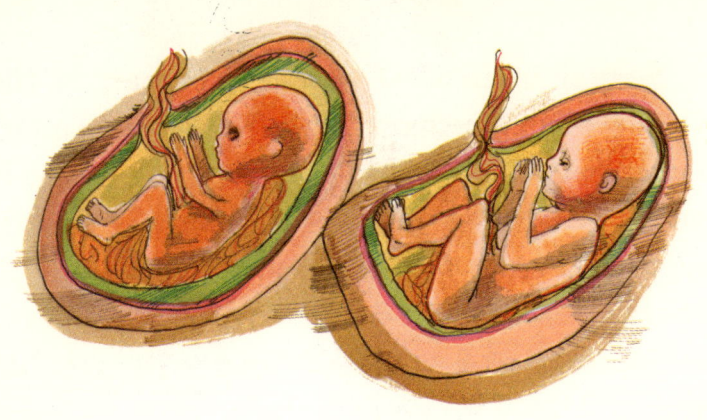

After about four months, the baby can begin to move in its sac. Mothers-to-be like this feeling. The mother's uterus stretches and makes more room for the baby. The shape of the mother's body changes. She wears *maternity* clothes because they are more comfortable for her changing shape.

During the nine months a baby is inside a mother's womb, it is fed through the *placenta*. The baby is connected to the lining of the mother's uterus by a long tube which is called the umbilical cord. This cord extends from the place where the baby's navel, or belly button, will be to the mother's uterus. It is like a small pipeline, and through it some of the baby's blood vessels run into the placenta. The blood vessels in the placenta help the oxygen in the mother's blood vessels take away the waste materials in the baby's blood stream.

The mother needs to eat good, nourishing food during these months because she is eating food for herself and for the baby. The baby can kick, and squirm, and move around. By the end of the nine months, the baby has grown so much that he can only turn from side to side. He usually settles in a head-down position. And it is in this position that the baby is born.

The way the baby grows for nine months is a wonderful part of God's plan. The way a baby is born is another wonderful part of God's plan.

The mother knows that it is time for the baby to be born when she feels the muscles in the uterus begin to push the baby out. Each push is called a contraction. She goes to the hospital when the contractions begin. We say this is when *labor* begins. After some time, the contractions will push the baby out through the vagina's opening between the legs of the mother. The opening of the vagina stretches to let the baby come out. During the labor, the muscles contract and rest, contract and rest.

As soon as a baby is born, the doctor or nurse may hold him upside down to help make his first breaths easier. At the same time that the baby is taking his first breath, his heart begins to pump blood to his lungs. The baby is no longer dependent on its mother for this part of life.

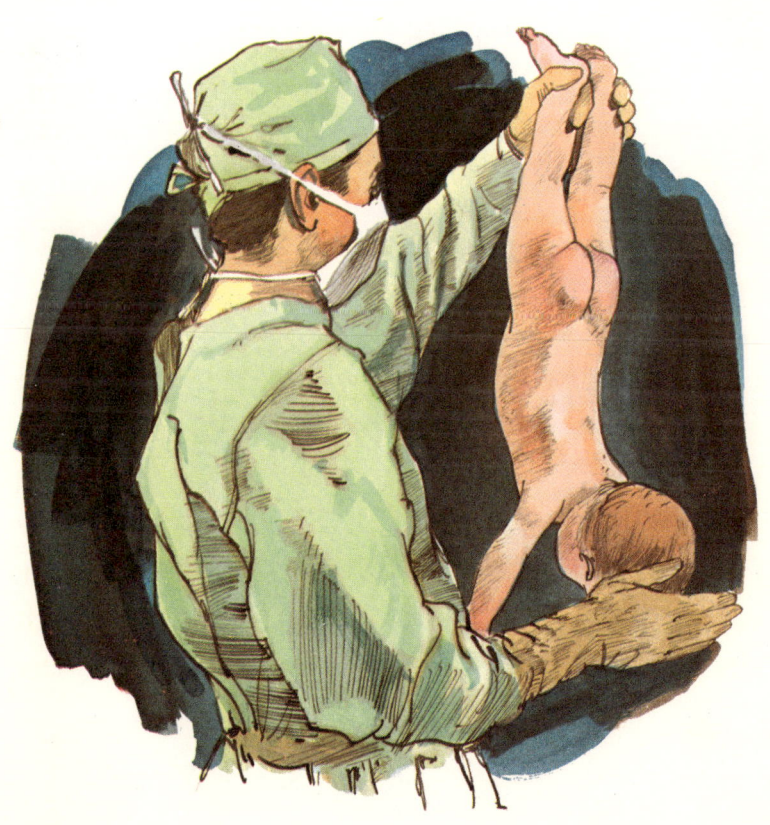

Feeding the New Born Baby

After you were born, your mother took you in her arms and held you. She loved you. You wanted to be with her, even though your eyes could hardly see and your brain was only starting to think.

Perhaps your mother fed you milk that was made in her *breasts*. The mother's breasts usually begin making milk soon after a baby is born. A baby sucks on the mother's nipples to get the milk. Sometimes a mother is unable to supply milk, but that is not a problem.

Many mothers use carefully prepared milk formulas to feed the baby by a bottle. Mothers of both breast-fed and bottle-fed babies cuddle them and hold them close to their bodies. By either method, the babies get enough food.

When you were newborn, you had to be fed every few hours and kept clean, warm, and dry. Most of the time, you just slept and grew. You are still growing and learning, and your body will keep on growing until you are about twenty years old. You will never stop learning things.

You have learned something about how you were born. You will learn even more as you grow older. Ask your parents anything you really want to know.

A Family Is Important

How many people are in your family? Is your family the same size as other families?

Families are many different sizes. Sometimes a grandmother or grandfather or other persons may live with the family. It doesn't matter what size the family is. The most important thing that members of a family get and give to one another is love. People need love just as they need food. If a baby does not receive love, the baby may grow up unhappy and unhealthy.

Do you remember when you were small? You probably thought about yourself most of the time. When children are very small, they think mostly about themselves. But as boys and girls grow older and receive love from their parents and from other people, they learn to give love as well as take it.

People have a longer childhood than any other kind of living thing. It takes about one year for a calf to become a full-grown cow and about three years for a colt to become a mature horse. It takes about twenty years for a child to become an adult. Even at twenty, and older, some adults don't act their age and may have a lot of growing up to do.

All through this long childhood, parents must give their children food, clothing, a place to live, and protection from harm. Parents must teach their children so that they will grow up to be happy and healthy and have respect for themselves and for other people as well.

Adolescence—Years of Change

Before you become a man or a woman, you will go through several years when many changes take place in your body, in your feelings, and in the things you enjoy doing. Changes in your ability to make wise decisions also happen. This time of growing up for boys and girls is called *adolescence.*

The rate of growth may be slow or fast. Have you ever heard of a growth spurt? This is a rapid increase in height and weight. A boy may grow six inches taller in one year. It takes a little time to make his body and his arms and legs graceful. This is one reason adolescence is called the "awkward stage." Life does not always run smoothly while boys and girls are learning to be men and woman. Just the same, adolescence is an exciting time when teen-agers enjoy many new experiences.

This spurt of growing happens to most girls when they are ten to twelve and to most boys when they are twelve to fourteen. Before this is over, small parts of the body called *glands* gradually bring about other body changes. These glands make certain kinds of liquids called hormones that are sent into the blood stream.

One of these glands, about as big as a small marble, is underneath your brain, safe inside your skull. This important gland is called the *pituitary*. This gland makes one hormone that determines the way your bones grow and how tall you grow. Another hormone helps your sex glands grow.

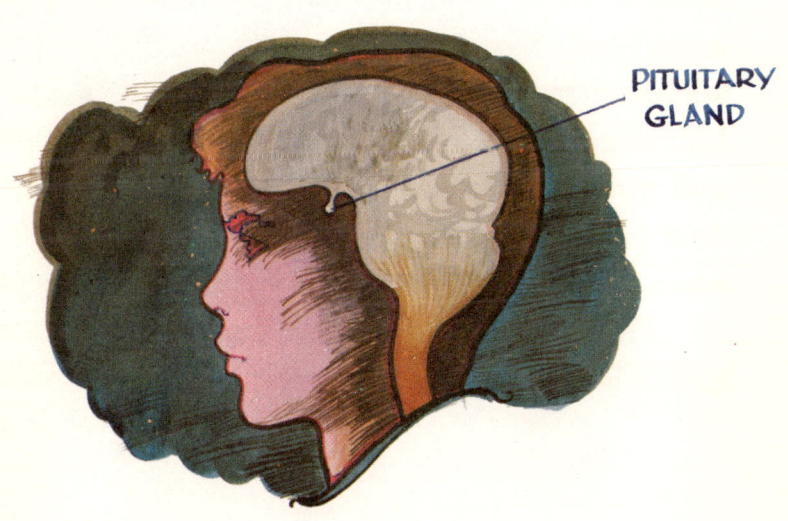
PITUITARY GLAND

Before boys and girls begin to have dates, they may sit together at church, they may walk to school together. This is a part of growing up. And it is important.

During adolescence, boys and girls begin to have dates. This is one way of getting to meet many different people. Dating is a practice for learning to understand and get along with the opposite sex. It is even getting ready for one day choosing a husband or a wife. So, it is important.

Learning to be comfortable with sexuality is part of growing up. Some people do not understand sex at all. Sex is a gift of God. It is important to learn about sex because each one of us is either male or female. This difference affects our lives in many ways. Sex is very wonderful and very important. Understanding about sex makes people proud and happy to be males or females. It makes people appreciate the differences between men and women, or boys and girls.

As you grow older, you will have more questions about sex. It is all right to ask questions about sex. Many people will be able to help you answer your questions. Your parents and your teachers may help you. So will your family doctor, school nurse, or a good, understanding neighbor. Your leaders at church may help you understand and appreciate more about sex, too.

Changes in Girls

A girl one day realizes that she has been growing taller and gaining weight. She may be taller than boys of the same age. She also finds that the form of her body is beginning to change. Her breasts develop and her hips be-

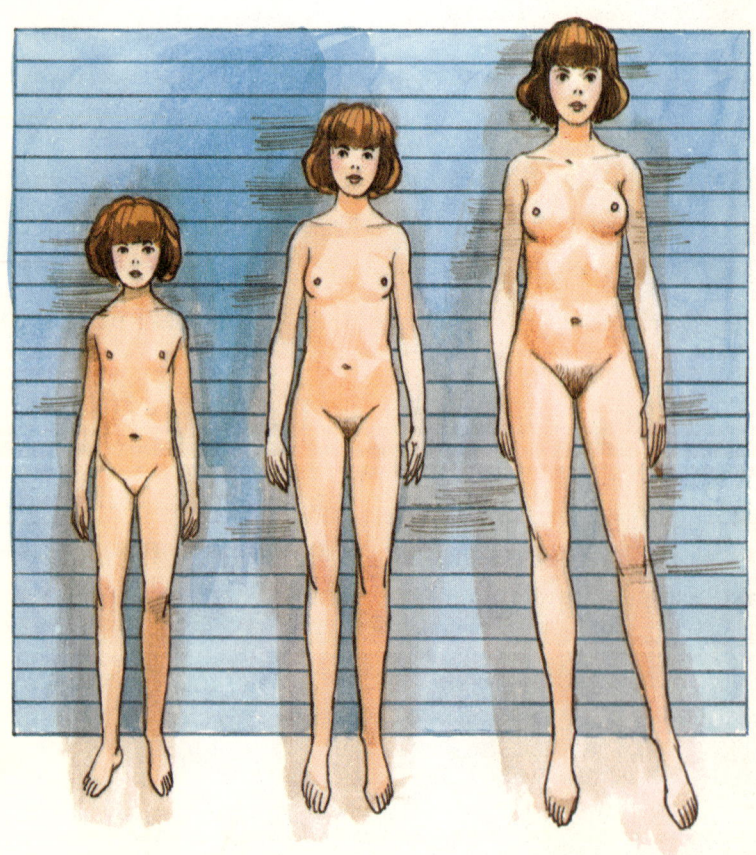

come fuller. Hair starts to grow under her arms and on the lower part of her abdomen. These changes happen slowly. Sometimes girls worry about the way their body is changing, but change is a part of God's plan.

When girls are about eleven, the hormone of the pituitary gland signals the ovaries, and they begin to grow. And then what happens? Girls begin to menstruate. After menstruation has started, a girl may expect it to happen about once a month. Young girls may skip a month or more quite often when they first begin to menstruate. Menstruation usually lasts just a few days each month. Since it comes at regular times, it is often called a "period."

Changes in Boys

The hormone of the pituitary gland also causes changes in boys. When they are about twelve, boys have an increased amount of this hormone.

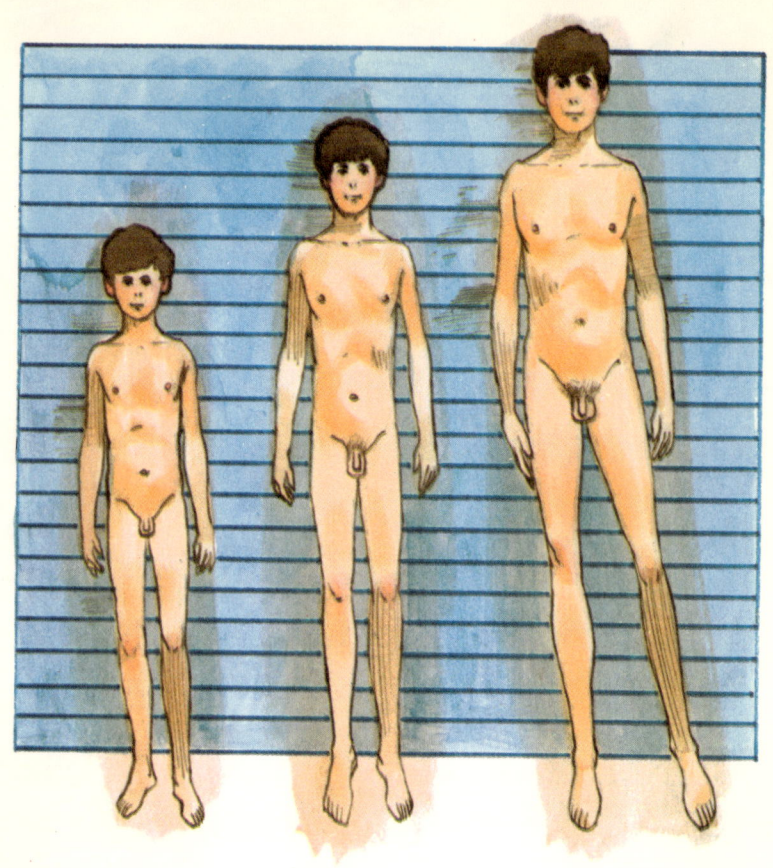

As a boy grows taller, he usually grows broader in his shoulders, and his sex organs—his penis and testicles—grow larger. His voice becomes deeper. Hair grows on the lower part of his abdomen, under his arms, and maybe on his chest and face. These changes take several years. Some boys grow faster than others. This is all right because God planned for each person to be different from any other person.

Soon after the changes begin, the testicles begin to produce sperm. The penis may occasionally become erect and firm. Sometimes semen passes out of the body through the penis. This is called a *seminal emission* or sometimes a nocturnal emission or "wet dream." A boy might wake up and find a white liquid in his shorts or pajamas. How often this happens, varies from boy to boy and from month to month. Some boys may never have them. They are never as regular as a girl's period. It is another sign that a boy is becoming a man and someday he may be a father.

All of these changes are a normal part of growing up. Before these changes occur, you are a child. After they happen, you are physically ready to be a parent. In our world, however, boys or girls need to develop in other ways before they should be fathers or mothers. They need to go to school, learn how to make a living, and learn how to take care of a home and family.

Masturbation

Perhaps you have heard of *masturbation*. It means handling one's own sex organs to cause a strong sexual feeling. In boys who are sexually mature this may result in an *ejaculation*. Ejaculation is a small amount of semen coming out of the penis. Masturbation is common among both boys and girls, but especially among boys.

You may have heard some strange things about masturbation. Doctors know that it does not cause mental illness, pimples, or use up all a boy's semen. None of these things is true. Perhaps the greatest harm is the guilt and fear that boys and girls feel if they masturbate. Most boys and girls masturbate less as they grow older and their lives are filled with friendships and interesting activities.

A Look Ahead

Maturing sexually is an important and interesting part of growing up, but other things also happen as a person becomes an adult.

When you were a small child, you played with both boys and girls. After you were older, if you are a boy, you probably played mostly with boys. If you are a girl, you played mostly with girls. This may be the way you choose friends now. As you grow older, you will choose some friends from the opposite sex.

While your body is growing and changing, your feelings are also changing. Sometimes you will feel happy. Sometimes you will feel sad. Sometimes you will make other people unhappy. It is not easy to understand how and why your feelings change. It will help to talk about your feelings with your parents or some grown-up friend.

An important question is how you feel about yourself while you are growing and changing.

The Bible has some good advice for boys and girls.

"Don't let people look down on you because you are young: see that they look up to you because you are an example to them in your speech and behavior, in your love and faith and sincerity. . . . Give your whole attention, all your energies, to these things, so that your progress is plain for all to see" (1 Timothy 4:12-15, Phillips).

From the very beginning God planned for sex to be a part of your life. If sex were bad, surely God would have made people in some other form. The story in the Bible about Adam and Eve helps us know that God planned for sex to be a part of life. It is a gift of God.

But God also planned for people to use their bodies in good and right ways. God planned for you, and he wants you to use your body in the best ways.

Part of God's wonderful plan is that boys and girls change and grow into men and women. You are a part of God's creation. God's creation is good!

Glossary

abdomen (AB-duh-men). The lower part of the trunk of the body; the belly.

adolescence (Ad-uh-LESS-uns). The time between childhood and adulthood which begins when the sex organs start to mature.

breast (BREST). One of the two glands on the upper chest of humans. In the female, the breasts produce milk shortly after the birth of a baby.

cell (SEL). The smallest unit of plant or animal bodies. A cell is often a microscopic bit of living material with a special function.

conception (kon-SEP-shun). The start of a new life through the union of a sperm cell with an egg cell; becoming pregnant.

egg (EG). A female sex cell, an ovum.

ejaculation (e-jak-u-LAY-shun). A discharge of semen through the penis.

erection (e-REK-shun). When the penis becomes firm and stands out from the body.

Fallopian tube (fa-LO-pe-an tube). There are two tubes, one leading from each ovary to the uterus.

fertilization (fer-tuh-luh-ZAY-shun). The union of the male and the female reproductive cell to form a new individual; to make pregnant.

gland (GLAND). An organ that forms one or more substances to be used in, or eliminated from, the body.

hormone (HOR-mohn). A substance produced by a gland and carried by the bloodstream to stimulate and regulate the activity of other parts of the body.

labor (LAY-ber). The exertion of childbirth as a mother's body pushes to give birth to her baby.

maternity (muh-TER-nih-tee). The quality or state of being a mother; motherhood.

masturbation (mass-ter-BAY-shun). Handling one's sex organs to have an intense sexual feeling. In boys who are sexually mature, an ejaculation, a discharge of semen, may occur.

menstruation (men-stroo-AY-shun). The periodic flow of blood, bits of uterine lining, and other materials from the uterus that takes place about every twenty-eight days in the human female, and lasts for four to seven days.

ovary (OH-vuh-ree). An almond-shaped female reproductive organ in which egg cells develop and sex hormones are produced.

ovulation (OH-vu-la-shun). The release of the egg each month from the ovary.

penis (PEE-niss). The male sex organ through which both urine and semen pass out of the body.

pituitary (pih-TYOO-ih-ter-ee). The body's master gland in the base of the brain. Its secretions control and regulate many other organs and thus influence most basic body functions.

placenta (pluh-SEN-tuh). A special network of blood vessels and tissue that develops on the lining of the uterus during pregnancy, in which food, oxygen, and wastes are exchanged between mother and child.

pregnant (PREG-nant). Carrying a growing baby in the uterus.

reproductive (ree-proh-DUK-tiv). Relating to or used in producing again, as in the creation of new life.

roles (ROLLS). How society expects us to act.

scrotum (SKROH-tum). The external sac of skin in which the testicles hang between the legs of a male.

semen (SEE-men). The male fertilizing fluid, composed of sperm and the whitish liquid in which they are suspended.

seminal emission (SEM-ih-nal eh-MISH-un). The discharge of semen from the penis. Also called nocturnal emission or "wet dreams."

sexual intercourse (SEK-shoe-al IN-tur-kors). The mating of humans, in which the penis of the male is placed within the vagina of the female.

sperm (SPERM). The male cell produced in the testicles for fertilizing the female egg.

testicle (TESS-ti-kul). The male reproductive gland in which sperm are produced.

uterus (YOOT-er-us). The hollow female organ for housing and feeding a baby during its development before birth.

vagina (vuh-JY-nuh). A passage leading from the uterus to the outside of the body; the birth canal.

womb (WUM). Another word for uterus.